simple
conjuring
tricks
for everyone

simple conjuring tricks
for everyone

★

julia thorley

Foreword by Michael Bailey
Past President of The Magic Circle

foulsham
LONDON • NEW YORK • TORONTO • SYDNEY

foulsham

The Publishing House, Bennetts Close, Cippenham,
Slough, Berkshire SL1 5AP, England

ISBN 0-572-03060-6

A CIP record for this book is available from the British Library

Artwork by Ruth Murray

Cover photograph © The Image Bank

Printed and bound in Great Britain by Cox & Wyman Ltd, Reading, Berkshire

Contents

Foreword

by Michael Bailey

Past President of The Magic Circle

The art of conjuring has been around a long time as records show that magicians were performing for the early Pharaohs in Egypt over 3,000 years ago. What's interesting is that magic is just as popular today, and people of all ages and nationalities still enjoy being amazed.

Many of us have had an urge at some time in our lives to perform a few baffling tricks, and from experience the best way to start is by reading books that explain the basic methods and offer tips on how to make the magic entertaining. *Simple Conjuring Tricks for Everyone* is an excellent manual for the beginner. It describes in clear detail how to perform and present a wide variety of easy-to-do tricks, using everyday objects or apparatus that can be made at very little cost.

If you study the text and illustrations – and put in the right amount of practice – you will discover that mystifying audiences isn't as difficult as you might think. Magic is an absorbing hobby, and you can receive as much satisfaction from learning the tricks as you can from presenting them before your friends and family. In time you could develop beyond the hobby stage and become proficient enough to join The Magic Circle – or even make conjuring your full-time career!

But please never forget that, after putting in enough practice and paying due attention to the presentation, it's the secret that's all-important. Don't be tempted to give away how these tricks are done. The effect on your audience is out of all proportion to the simplicity of the methods employed, and once the secret is out the fun of being fooled is gone forever.

I hope you will get many hours of enjoyment from reading, learning, and presenting the magic in this book.

1.

Introduction to the basics of conjuring

This book is for anyone who wants to begin a study of the art of the conjuror or illusionist. The tricks presented here are for the most part simple to do but impressive to watch. For many of them you won't need expensive equipment, just bits and pieces that can be found in the home or bought fairly easily. In the few instances where more elaborate apparatus is required, this can either be made without too much difficulty or bought from good toy shops or specialist magic shops.

The tricks and illusions described in this basic introduction to conjuring might not ensure your admission to the Magic Circle, but they will without any doubt provide plenty of entertainment and puzzlement for your family and friends.

But first, some basics.

PRACTICE MAKES PERFECT

The key to being a successful conjuror is to practise, practise, practise. Select half a dozen tricks that appeal to you most, then practise until you can perform them with complete ease, without looking at what you're doing.

An audience looks first at the performer, then at what he or she is doing and then at whatever real or imaginary object the conjuror chooses to look at with a definite gaze. So as soon as you have mastered the movements required by the trick itself, practise them in front of a mirror and don't look at your hands or their reflection. The only exception to this is when you are learning a new trick, when you might need to check the actions of your hands as they will appear to your audience.

You need to be able to control your hands, so that while they are apparently moving freely you can actually conceal something behind them until the time comes for that object to be 'revealed' to the audience.

Development of hand control is facilitated by deliberate practice. For example, hold a coin flat between the third and fourth fingers of your hand while holding, say, a button in the palm of your hand, by means of light pressure with the second finger, while manipulating a pencil – or preferably the 'magic wand' – between the thumb and first finger. Practise with both hands in this manner using various objects whenever you have an idle moment, and you will be surprised how the adaptability and flexibility of your hands develops.

PALMING

Palming is the act of concealing an item in your hand while other operations are going on, all without anyone being aware of your actions. It is a highly useful accomplishment and one that is not difficult, after a little practice. Practise with a playing card. The palmed card is simply clipped between the ball of the thumb and the top joints of the fingers.

To get the card into position, hold the pack, with the card to be palmed on top, in the left hand and cover with the right lengthways. With the thumb of the left hand push the card about 2cm (³/₄in) off the pack, and then with the fingers of the left hand underneath and right round the pack push the card upwards into the palm of your right hand. Bend the hand and the card will remain out of sight as long as you keep your fingers

Palming a card

11

close together, knuckles uppermost. Try sitting with a card in this position while you are watching TV, and it will soon become so comfortable that you don't betray its presence by holding your hand awkwardly.

To palm a coin, begin by holding it lightly between the fingertips. Turn the fingers inward with a quick movement and press the coin against the palm, and at the same moment contract the palm so that the flesh grips over the edge of the coin. Extend the fingers naturally and move the hand about freely, but without letting the palm of the hand become visible to the audience. There is more guidance on manipulating coins on page 41.

The best way to become efficient is to go steady at the start, get the action and the palm grip correct, then gradually work up the speed. Don't try to work too quickly at the start; speed and dexterity will soon be acquired by repeated practice.

Support your palming by clever patter and misdirection; that is, attract the attention of the audience to one thing while you do another.

PATTER

Develop your own style of patter to enhance your performance. Don't try to be formal, if this doesn't come naturally to you. Similarly, don't try to tell jokes as you go along if this is going to distract you. Experiment with various styles of addressing your audience, decide what works for you and stick with it. There are times when you will need to use your patter to divert attention from what your hands are doing. Similarly, wear clothes that are comfortable but that allow for the possibility of concealing cards and other props about your person. Black is a good colour because it makes an effective backdrop for concealment. Similarly, a suit, complete with waistcoat, looks good and offers the option of lots of pockets. Wide sleeves are a must.

Whatever style you adopt, remember to speak clearly and distinctly, addressing those towards the back of the room and turning from one to another, so that all are interested. Doing this helps you to throw your voice well forward so that everyone can hear you. Much of the woodenness of the amateur speaker is overcome by addressing individual members of the audience in turn. After a time, you will find that you can speak clearly, while moving your head in various directions and following with your eyes a movement elsewhere in the room.

When addressing your audience, whatever happens, *never* lose your temper! Always have a smile and a joke at hand for emergencies, and remember that the most vicious critic who 'knows all about your tricks' will subside like a burst balloon under a little gentle, good-humoured teasing.

Never attempt to shout down the audience. If they are laughing, clapping and enjoying themselves, let them continue in that happy state. Once the hubbub subsides sufficiently, start speaking in a quiet, ordinary voice and the audience will at once become attentive, because they will all want to listen and hear what you are saying.

APPARATUS

An evening's entertainment in the home and quite a good show on the stage can be given by any reasonably expert amateur, simply by working magic that requires neither trick apparatus nor the preparation of any special devices. Many of the tricks given in this book have been chosen with that object in view, but for those who like to use special props, a number of inexpensive trick pieces are described, along with hints given for making the apparatus. Some of the tricks in this book require items to be borrowed from the audience: coins, handkerchiefs and so on. However, it is as well to have all the necessary items to hand, just in case none can be borrowed.

Magic Wand

A wand of some kind – either plain or 'trick' – is almost essential. The audience will expect you to have one; it is rather like a badge of office. You can buy a wand from a magic supplies shop, or make one.

Prepare a wand by painting matt black a piece of smooth wooden rod about 6mm ($\frac{1}{4}$in) in diameter and 20–30cm (8–12in) long. Next get a piece of black silk thread about 20cm (8in) long, tie a non-slipping loop at each end of it, slip the rod into these loops and draw the thread out straight along the wand.

Now try this little bit of 'magic'. Explain that by your powers of magnetism you can raise the wand and make it perform in the air. Run the fingers of your right hand along the wand – with magic 'passes' – and gradually raise the wand to a nearly vertical position. You do this by working a finger of the right hand under the thread, the passes giving you the chance to do this unobserved. Then repeat the performance with the left hand, but this time get the thread over the back of the hand and extend a finger to press against the wand. Then, if you keep the wand towards the audience and the back of your hand away from them, the wand will appear to be floating in the air. At the completion of the trick, draw the wand through the hand and let the thread fall – unobserved – to the floor.

Another trick with a wand is to insert a fine needle in one end, with the sharp end of the needle sticking out about 6mm

(¼in). Don't forget it is there! 'Balance' the wand on an apple, or upon an egg on which a little pad of white wax has been smeared so as not to show. The sharp end of the needle will grip enough to hold the wand upright if it is reasonably well balanced. Afterwards, discreetly pull out the needle and use another wand for the rest of your act.

Conjuror's Hat

Another traditional adjunct to any conjuror is a hat of sorts from which to produce a rabbit, enormous lengths of coloured paper or almost anything that takes your fancy. A top hat is the best because of its size, but a bowler can also be used. There need be nothing special about the hat. All that really matters is that you acquire the knack of 'loading' it without being observed. Most conjurors have their own pet method.

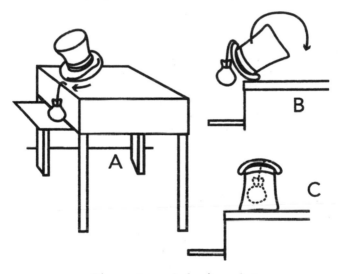

Three stages in loading a hat

One way is to have a narrow shelf at the back of your table, with the 'load' standing on it. The hat is shown to be 'perfectly empty', placed upside-down on the table, and then tilted over as at A in the figure on page 15, so that it engages a hook attached to a short thin string tied to the load. The hat is then tilted towards the audience (B), in such a way that the load is swung upwards and into the hat (C), which by this time will again be standing upside-down.

Another way, shown below, is to have the load suspended by a light thread attached to any convenient part of the table or elsewhere out of sight of the audience. Bow extravagantly to the audience and, with a graceful sweep of the hat, scoop up the load behind the table, catch it by the fingers and tilt it into the hat.

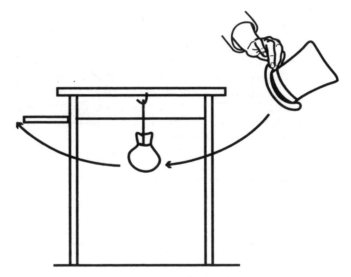

Sweeping in the load

Still another way is casually to knock the hat over with the right arm, catch it in mid-air, sweep it deftly round and on to the table, but, as you do so, you must equally deftly drop in the 'load' with the left hand.

Table

A table of some sort is essential as a place on which to put the various things you will need. Any regular table will do, so long as it is light and slender in style. As your conjuring skills progress, you might want to make or buy a conjuror's table with traps and secret pockets, but you won't need anything that sophisticated for the tricks in this book.

Magic Gloves

'Vanishing' gloves can make a very simple and impressive introduction, and can be easily made with a pair of comfortably fitting white fabric gloves. To the middle of the front portion, nearest the wrist, sew a piece of thin white elastic thread measuring about 30cm (12in) in length. Make a loop at the free end and pass it over a strong safety-pin. Fix the safety-pin securely inside your coat sleeve, at a suitable distance from the cuff, so that when the glove has 'vanished', it is well out of sight.

2.

Simple but effective tricks

You might think that some of the tricks in this section are so simple that no one could possibly be fooled by them. You couldn't be more wrong. A receptive audience expects to be mystified and while you might come across the occasional clever-clogs who likes to spoil things, most people will go along with the act and are happy to be deceived.

Nevertheless, even these tricks need to be practised so that you can perform them deftly and with confidence. Once you have mastered the sleight of hand, you can work on your patter so that a selection of these basic tricks can be used to create a pleasing show for family and friends.

EXTINGUISHING A CANDLE WITH AN EMPTY BOTTLE

Simple physics is the secret to this trick. You will need a dry, clean, empty bottle and a lighted candle.

1. While out of sight of the audience, place your thumb over the opening of the bottle, so that only a small aperture is left; then blow lustily into the bottle. Compress and secure the air within it by pressing the thumb firmly over the opening.

The sudden release of air extinguishes the candle

2. Bring the bottle near to the lighted candle, lift your thumb slightly and the rush of air from the bottle will blow out the candle.

Take care that the candle wick is low and the flame small at the time the trick is performed.

ADHESIVE PENCIL

How can you make a pencil stick to the palm of your hand? This first trick has already deluded thousands of people, and will probably do the same to thousands more.

1. Hold up your left hand, palm facing the audience and clutching a pencil in a horizontal manner. Now, tell the audience that, by severely straining the muscles, you can exert a mysterious adhesive property. Once, you will add, you nearly dislocated your wrist while performing this trick so to prevent reoccurrence, you will grip the wrist tightly with the right hand. This you do, with the thumb at the front.

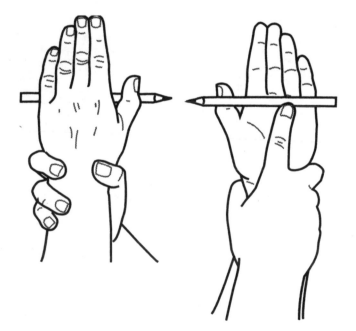

What the audience sees (left) and how the pencil is supported

2. Now, without apparently altering the grip on the wrist, revolve the left hand so that the back comes to view, with the pencil protruding from either side.
3. Slowly straighten out your fingers and bring the left-hand thumb round to the front of the pencil so that it no longer supports the pencil. In fact, none of the fingers is supporting it, now that they are stretched out. What is it that keeps the pencil from falling? Why, your adhesive properties, of course!
4. Actually, when you rotate your left hand within the right-hand grip, you quickly raise the index finger of the right hand to support the pencil, unknown to the audience

You might think that the audience would at once notice how this trick is done. But you'll be surprised to find that the onlooker does not notice the absence of the index finger.

MAGIC RING

This is a surprisingly easy trick, yet it is a very effective one. You can make a ring climb up and down your magic wand at your command.

☛ Before you begin, attach a black thread to the top of your wand and continue it down the wand on the side away from the audience. Once the trick is under way, you will hold the wand in one hand and the end of the thread in the other.
1. Borrow an ordinary gold ring from a member of the audience and hand it round for inspection.
2. Slip the ring over the wand, which you hold vertically. The ring, of course, falls down and rests on your hand.

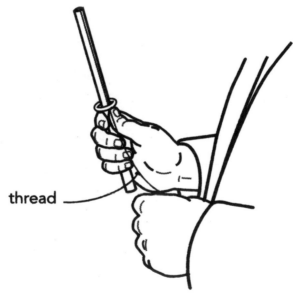

thread

Pull on the thread to move the ring

3. Ask everybody to watch carefully. The ring begins to climb up and up the wand. After a while, it descends a little, then commences the climb again. When it has travelled up and down once or twice, command it to do your bidding. Say, 'Up!' and up it goes. Say, 'Down!' and down it goes. Say, 'Stop!' and it stops. Amazing: it will do whatever you ask!
4. The secret is that by discreetly varying the distance between your hand and the wand, the tension in the thread causes the ring to rise or fall.

You must wear a black jacket to perform this trick, so that the thread is obscured.

RING AND EGG TRICK

This trick consists of wrapping a borrowed wedding ring in a handkerchief, making the ring disappear and discovering it in an egg, selected by one of the audience at random from several on a dish.

- ☛ To prepare for the trick, sew a wedding ring into one corner of a handkerchief, and melt a little white wax – no more than 6mm (¹/₄in) – into the bottom of an eggcup. You will also need a button hook or other hook on a piece of wire.
1. To begin the trick, ask to borrow a wedding ring from a member of the audience.
2. Shake the handkerchief to show that it is empty, of course holding the corner with the wedding ring in it. Then pretend to wrap the borrowed ring in the handkerchief, but actually palm it and wrap up the wedding ring that is already sewn to the handkerchief.
3. Ask someone in the audience to feel the handkerchief and confirm that the ring is there. While this is being done, slip the borrowed ring into the wax in the bottom of the eggcup, setting the ring upright.

The ring is secured in the wax

4. Take back the handkerchief and show that the ring has vanished by shaking it while holding the corner containing the ring. Ask someone to give you one of the eggs, take it and press it well down into the eggcup, thus forcing the ring through the shell. Break the top of the egg and, with the button hook, draw out the ring. Rinse it in a finger bowl, wipe it dry and hand it back to the owner.

The key to this trick is subtle misdirection.

SELF-TYING SCARVES

Two coloured silk scarves are exhibited and may be handed round for close inspection. They are then thrown up into the air, and come down tied together. They are once more tossed into the air, and on descending it is noticed they are single, and no trace of a knot is to be seen.

☛ Before you begin, place a small, thin elastic band over the thumb and first finger of the right hand, keeping the thumb and first finger as close together as possible.

1. With the left hand, pick up the two scarves, and hand them to one of the audience for scrutiny. Take them back, taking care to catch hold of one corner of each, and promptly place them between the thumb and first finger of the right hand, immediately below the elastic band.

2. Standing with your left side towards the audience, drop your right hand slightly, and in that moment allow the elastic band to slip from its previous position and to encircle the scarves. Throw them into the air and they appear to be tied.

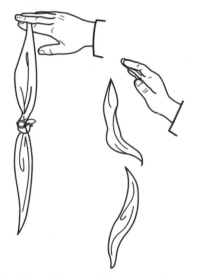

The 'knot' is actually an elastic band

3. As they fall to the floor, gently pick up a corner of one scarf and the other scarf will hang from it, as if they were tied together.
4. Throw the scarves into the air a second time. This time, give the scarf that you are holding a sudden pull just as it leaves your hand. This will at once free the elastic band, and as the scarves fall down the audience will notice that no knot – or sign of one – is to be found.

A very knotty problem indeed!

MAGIC PAPER RINGS

This simple trick is always amusing and mystifying. Make sure you lead your audience to the right conclusion with your beguiling patter!

1. Take a strip of paper about 90cm (36in) long and 2.5–5cm (1–2in) wide. Draw a pencil line along the whole length of one side of the paper and at about the middle of its width, then paste together the two ends so that the pencil marks come together, face to face, thus forming a ring.
2. Actually, this method of joining the ends gives a single twist somewhere in the length of the paper; but if this is noticed, pass it off to the audience as of no consequence.
3. Now start to cut along the pencil line with a pair of scissors. Don't say what the result of this will be but lead the audience to expect two separate rings. When you have finished cutting the paper, however, you will not have two separate rings but one large ring twice the size of the original ring.

A twist in the paper will give you two rings

4. At this result say something about the paper being bewitched, and try again with another strip of paper of the same dimensions, but this time discreetly make two twists, then cut as before. When you have finished you will not have one large ring, but two rings, one linked to the other.

For greater effect and to raise a bigger laugh, invite a volunteer from the audience to do the actual cutting. It is not necessary to pencil in the cutting line once you have acquired the knack of giving the paper the necessary twist.

TUMBLING DICE

This satisfying trick will make you look very smart, but in fact it is just simple maths.

1. Take a sheet of glass, place three dice on it, and rattle them about so that they tumble over and over and then come to rest. While doing this, stand on a chair and look down on the dice.
2. As the dice are tumbling about, ask for one member of the audience to come out and look up through the glass at the bottom faces of the dice. Naturally, your elevated position makes it quite clear that you cannot see the bottom faces.
3. Ask him to count up the pips on the three bottom faces, without mentioning the total. Immediately after you have finished your instructions, cease rattling the dice about. As quickly as possible tell the audience what they add up to and ask the person who is looking upwards if you are correct. He will confirm that you are.

Simple maths dictates that the bottom faces add up to 7

4. This is the secret. All dice, if they are of regulation pattern, are numbered in the same way. This means that if you look at the top faces of the dice, add them up and subtract their total from 21, this will give the total of the bottom faces. For example, say the top faces are 3, 6 and 5. This adds up to 14. Subtract 14 from 21 and you get 7.

Repeat this a couple of times more to prove that it wasn't a fluke, then move on smartly to another trick – before the audience works out what is going on.

RED, WHITE AND BLUE CANDLES

The mystery in this trick depends on careful preparation but once that is done it is virtually foolproof.

☞ Before the show, you take three ordinary candles and press a small magnet into the bottom of one, into the middle of another and into the tip of the third.

1. To work the trick, take the three prepared candles and wrap each in a different colour paper, apparently at random. Actually, you put the blue round the candle with the magnet at the bottom: B for blue and bottom. Put the white paper round the candle with the magnet at the tip, near the wick: W for white and wick. The red paper goes round the candle loaded in the middle.

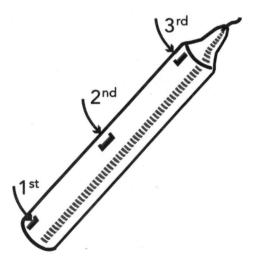

A magnet is concealed, one in each candle in each of these positions

2. The three wrapped candles are spread out on a little table in front of your audience.

3. 'Ladies and gentlemen,' you say, 'I have here three very mysterious candles. They are just ordinary candles, nothing unusual about them, except that they are wound round with papers of our national colours. I need two volunteers to come and blindfold me.'

4. When you have assured your audience that you cannot see, explain that you are now going to identify the colour of the candles.

5. Ask one of your volunteers to pass the candles to you one at a time, and as they do so to give each a good twist, lest you are able to identify it by the way it is wrapped. While the choice is being made, you walk up and down in a mysterious manner. Take the opportunity to slip your hand into your pocket and carefully work a thin strip of iron into position between the first and second fingers of the right hand.

6. The candles are handed to you one by one, and, of course, you announce which is which in a clear voice. You can do this because you run your hand along the candle. When the iron passes over the magnet, it becomes slightly agitated, so you can instantly identify the colour.

Be aware that your volunteers may well try to trick you. Just because you identify the first two as red and white, don't assume that the next must be blue. It is quite likely to be red or white again.

STRIKING MATCH

This trick is a 'filler' that you can drop into your act when you have an odd moment. We all know that a safety match will only strike on its own box. Not true: you can strike it on your shoe.

☛ Before your performance, put a very thin layer of glue on the instep of your shoe and then scrape the black striking material from two or three boxes on it. It would even do to stick a part of the actual strip from a box on the instep.

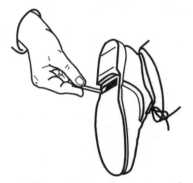

Conceal a striking strip on the instep of your shoe

1. Let us suppose that you are about to perform some mysterious feat and, while filling in a moment, you decide to light a candle. Get out your box of matches and instead of striking the match on the box, deliberately lift up your foot and do the striking of the sole of your shoe. The match lights!

2. 'Funny matches, these,' you remark to the audience, and invite someone to come and see if they can light a match on their shoe. Of course, nobody can. Then, in case it may be thought that you had a specially prepared match, ask your volunteer to pick one at random out of the box and hand it to you. When he does so, you strike it on your shoe and offer a candle to him, with the lighted match all ready.

You chose the instep of your shoe because you do not wear it away when you walk.

MAGNETISED STICK

Not really a trick, but a tricky piece of fun nonetheless. To perform this stunt you need a walking stick or similar and a piece of smooth cardboard.

1. Balance the stick on the back of a chair.
2. Then hand the cardboard to your 'victim' and bet him that he can't make the stick move on the back of the chair without touching it with this card or anything else, and without fanning it or blowing upon it. Unless he knows the secret, he won't be able to.

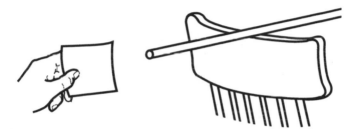

Static causes the stick to move

3. When he gives up, take the cardboard in your own hands. Rub it briskly on your jacket for a few minutes, saying as you do so that you want to remove his fingermarks. Then quickly hold the card near one end of the balanced stick. Slowly begin to move the card to one side of the stick. The stick will follow the card!

The reason, of course, is that the static created by rubbing the card on your jacket attracts the stick.

FANTASY FIVEPENCE

This is a downright silly trick that will cause roars of laughter.

1. Take a 5p coin and press it against your forehead. When it has stuck there, try to make it fall off and then catch it in one of your waistcoat pockets, which you hold wide open. This will take some practice: don't try to perform this trick until you can do it successfully.
2. Demonstrate this remarkable talent to a group of friends and one of them is sure to want to try it for himself. So let him have a go.

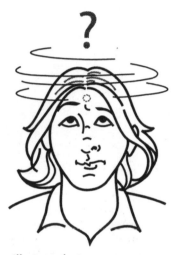

Your victim will struggle to remove a non-existent coin

3. Take the coin, press it against the forehead of your victim, holding it there for a few moments. Then whip it away. Your friend will not know it is gone but will make all sorts of grimaces in an endeavour to dislodge it. The fact is, he can feel the impression instead of the coin. It is only when the onlookers roar with laughter that he will guess the truth.

You can use this trick to deflate an overenthusiastic audience member.

BALL IN A JAR

This is not a trick so much as a piece of skill.

1. Take a large glass jar, one with some constriction at the neck, and stand it upside-down on the table and over a ball. The ball must be considerably smaller than the mouth of the jar. Now ask if there is anybody in the audience who can carry the jar and the ball round the stage or room and bring it back to the table. The ball must not be touched and the jar may not be turned bottom downwards. Naturally, the ball must not be allowed to fall. If anybody does try, the probability is that he will not get far!

Keep the jar moving and the ball will not fall

2. The way to do it is to grasp the jar with both hands opened wide; then draw the jar to the edge of the table, and the moment the table is left, to lower the jar a little but very rapidly, and then to keep up a continuous shaking movement that causes the ball to revolve round and round inside.

When you know how, it is not difficult.

MAGIC LADDER

Audiences greatly appreciate any act in which folded paper is torn or cut in such a way that, when opened, it makes some curious object or pattern. Accordingly it is advisable to practise two or three stunts of this nature. Try this one.

1. Take four pages from a broadsheet newspaper, fold them lengthways across the middle of the pages and tear into two pieces of equal size. You now have two long strips that are fairly narrow. Discard one of them for the moment and hold the other up for the audience to see. Turn it round so that the back is also inspected. Make absolutely no comments while doing this. Your silence will cause the audience to wonder what you are going to do.
2. Now stand in front of the strip and, with your hands behind your back, slowly wind it up, while facing the audience. In winding the paper do not make it too tight or bunch it.
3. With your hands still behind you, tear a section out of the roll as shown below, then slightly bend the roll.

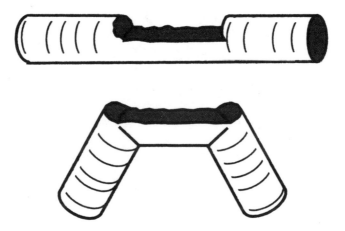

The two stages in the construction of the Magic Ladder

4. At this point, reveal the shape to the audience for the first time; then, without wasting a moment, grip the two lower ends of the bent roll with the left hand and, with the right, pull out the tops of the roll. You will have to pull each one alternately, a little at a time. When extended to its full length the roll becomes a long ladder with flat rungs complete. Stand it against the background of the stage and it will be sufficiently rigid to stay there, without crumpling up.

It is a really marvellous piece of paper-tearing.

PALM TREE

This paper trick is very impressive and needs quite a bit of practice to get right.

1. Take a complete sheet from a broadsheet newspaper and fold it across the columns so that you make three equal widths. Tear twice and use only one of the pieces.
2. Place the paper behind you and roll it up, not too tightly. When this is done, and while the paper is still out of sight, tear down the roll four or five times from one end almost to the middle. The tears may be straight or crinkled, whichever you prefer.
3. Now, show the roll to the audience and, gripping the untorn end with the left hand, pull one of the innermost torn sections. As it comes up it forms a column, which is the tree trunk with numerous flaps of paper on all sides. These are the branches or leaves.

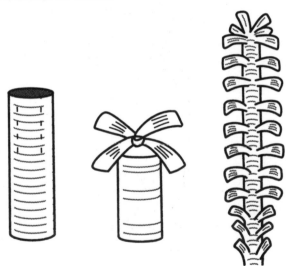

Making a Palm Tree

Pause to give your audience time to appreciate your handiwork then move straight on to the following trick.

HERE WE GO ROUND THE MULBERRY BUSH

1. Take one of the strips of paper discarded from Palm Tree, on the previous page. Fold it down the middle lengthwise, and tear. You now have a fairly long, narrow strip.
2. Pleat it into sections about 7.5cm (3in) wide. Using scissors, cut the paper to make the shape of one half of a person, but be very careful to arrange for a horizontal arm to reach to the extreme edge of the pleated sections of paper.
3. Unfold, and you will have a long length of little people, all holding hands.

Once mastered, these paper tricks can form a simple but amusing self-contained routine.

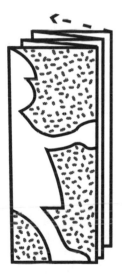

The folded paper, showing potential cut lines

3.

Tricks with coins

Tricks with coins have the advantage that most of them can be presented without any preliminary preparation; they can be performed anywhere at a moment's notice and are always effective.

Work on your dexterity whenever you have an idle moment, until you can manipulate the coins with fingertip control and without looking at your hands. Coins are small so your audience will be paying close attention: don't let them see how the trick is done!

As with card tricks, the best way to begin is to master the art of palming. The process for doing this is explained on the pages that follow.

PALMING A COIN

Every conjuror worthy of the name must know how to palm coins and other small articles in order to be able to get rid of them, or suddenly produce them from apparently nowhere when performing certain tricks. Palming can be done as an act in itself or, what is more usual, as an essential part of other tricks. To do it well, constant practice is essential, and any prospective performer should go over the movements dozens of times before trying them in public.

Naturally, coins of all denominations must be palmed on occasions; but it is advisable to practise with a 10p coin, since it is easily handled and of good weight and thickness.

Stage one

The first thing is to learn how to hold a coin in the palm of the hand, comfortably and without dropping it.

To do this, place the coin centrally on the palm and just crease up the hand a little. Then wave the hand about and endeavour to move the fingers. On the first occasion the coin will be sure to fall, but a little practice will reveal that there is one spot on the palm that affords a better grip than any other and, when it has been located, the holding becomes relatively easy. In less than ten minutes' practice it will probably be found that the coin can be held firmly and the fingers moved in a natural manner.

A coin can be held quite securely in a slightly creased hand

Stage two

1. Now practise the art of pretending to transfer the coin from one hand to the other when actually it remains in the same hand throughout.
2. Hold the coin between the thumb and first and second fingers of the right hand.
3. Quickly take away the thumb and direct the coin by means of the fingers to the palm, where it is gripped.

The coin has apparently vanished, but is actually palmed in the right hand

4. Straighten out the fingers of the right hand at once and at the same time bring the outstretched fingers of the left hand towards them.
5. Close the fingers of the left hand in a pretence that they are clutching the coin. Make a show of having the right hand open, but with the palm containing the coin turned away from the audience.

Stage three

The third step is to know how to make a coin disappear. There are several ways of doing this.

1. Hold the coin between the thumb and first and second fingers of the right hand.
2. Pose the hand slightly upwards so that the coat sleeve is open to receive the coin as it falls. Note that a stiffened shirt cuff is the best sort to wear for this purpose.

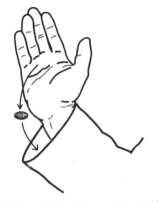

The spinning coin is dropped into the cuff

3. Twirl the fingers in much the same way as you would when spinning a top. This action rotates the coin and on letting it go it darts rapidly into the cuff, where it remains out of sight. Of course, a certain amount of skill is needed to direct the coin into the coat and not let it fly on to the floor. This comes with practice.

An alternative method is to bore a fine hole in a coin and thread a piece of elastic through it. The other end of the elastic is tied to the arm, inside the coat, and its length is such that it is not visible. When about to palm a coin, strain the elastic so that the coin can be seen; wrap a handkerchief around it, making a great show of the business; then give a sudden jerk, whip out the handkerchief into the air, release the coin so that it flies up the sleeve, and hold the open hands up to show that there is no deception. The coin has vanished into thin air!

A quick movement will jerk the coin out of the handkerchief and up the sleeve

This plan of making a coin disappear is a very useful one, as it may be applied with equal success to other small objects.

SOFT COIN

Try this feat on an unsuspecting audience when you want a laugh, or when you wish to score over a troublesome spectator.

1. Ask for the loan of a 10p coin. Look at it suspiciously then, holding it upwards a little, and facing towards the audience, say something about it being a 'peculiar coin, as soft as putty', and at the same time proceed to bend and twist it about.
2. All you do is to place both thumbs behind the coin, bend over the first fingers at the knuckles so that the fingertips come just at the bottom of the coin and steady it against the thumb tips. The coin, as seen by the audience, now appears to be firmly gripped but is, in fact, only held between the tips of the fingers and thumbs.

An optical illusion – the movement of your fingers makes it look as though the coin is bending

3. If now you 'bend' the coin, by moving your hands in exactly the same way that you would move them if the coin were made of lead. The effect to the audience will be that the coin is actually being distorted.

You can bend, stretch or twist a coin by making the corresponding movements with the appropriate commentary.

CHANGING 5P INTO 10P

This is a simple and easy trick, but one that is very effective when performed with a suitable accompaniment of patter.

☛ Before you begin, secretly place a 10p coin between the second and third fingers of the right hand, and keep the hand palm downwards so as to conceal the coin.

1. Borrow a 5p coin from a member of the audience and offer to double his money for him. Take the 5p coin in the left hand.

2. With a quick motion of the left hand, bring it under the right and stop it quickly. This has the effect of shooting the 5p into the right sleeve of your jacket. At the same moment, release the 10p and allow it to drop unseen into the left hand. Immediately show the 10p to the audience, but do not part with it!

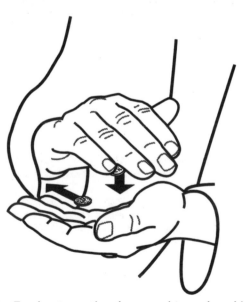

The 5p shoots up the sleeve and is replaced by the 10p

3. To restore the 5p, drop the right arm, thus allowing the coin to fall unseen into the right hand while the audience are looking at the 10p. Make as if to give the 10p to the person who lent the 5p, but substitute the latter coin, making a passing movement of the hands as if to pick up the 10p with the right hand.

This takes a bit of practice, but once mastered it is very effective.

THE REAPPEARING COIN

This trick is a little more challenging and there is a certain amount of preparation needed, but its performance isn't too difficult for the novice.

☛ You will need three tumblers of uniform size, for which you should make three coloured paper covers to slip over the glasses and hide them from the view of the audience.

☛ Cut a strip off one end of a large sheet of smooth brown paper and prepare two discs. Glue these over the mouth of two of the tumblers. When the gum is dry, trim off any overhanging edges of brown paper. You will now have two tumblers each with a disc of brown paper across their mouths, one tumbler in its natural state and three paper covers. You also need three coins of the same denomination.

1. Place the remainder of the brown paper on the tablecloth, 'just to prevent it being soiled'. Put down one of the coins and place the unprepared tumbler over it; put the other two tumblers one on each side of it, and while doing so, slip a coin under each. The brown paper discs are, of course, invisible and hide the coins.

Lifting the cover on a tumbler with a disc will create the illusion that the coin has disappeared

2. Put all three covers over the glasses, and 'pass' the coin to the right, revealing it by lifting the cover and the glass. Put the glass and its cover back on the table and transfer the coin to the middle glass, showing this by removing the cover. Ring the changes on the three glasses a few times to keep up the mystery. Be sure to remember to lift the outer glasses to reveal the coin, and to lift only their covers when the coin is to 'disappear'.

10P THAT GOES

Of course, it is not at all difficult to make 10p go – what is difficult is to keep it. At least, that is what you will tell your audience. You apparently make a coin disappear at your elbow only for it to reappear at your neck.

1. You borrow a 10p coin, then, bending your left arm, you rub the coin on your elbow until it disappears, and your hand is empty. At this point, you will show a pair of wide-open hands in order to prove that you really have rubbed the coin away.
2. Next you look amazed and say, 'Ah, I can feel it. Will someone come and remove it from its hiding place? It's between my collar and my neck.' Someone comes forward and finds it exactly where you said it was. Naturally, the audience is baffled.
3. So how is it done? At the start of the trick, you make a great fuss in order to emphasise the fact that the coin is in your right hand and then you commence to rub. But you are a little clumsy and allow the coin to drop out of your hand and roll on the floor. Naturally, you say something to the effect that you are sorry, and you make the audience think that that part of the performance was unintentional (though, of course, it was actually planned).

While the audience is watching your right hand,
surreptitiously drop the coin from your left

4. Bend down and make for a spot on the floor about 45cm (18in) to the right of where the coin is resting. With your right hand, you pretend to pick it up. But, at the same time, you support yourself, while bending, with the left hand – an action that seems a perfectly natural one – and the left hand just touches the ground where the coin is lying.

5. Without any show, you pick up the coin with the left hand, and then proceed with the trick. You bend the left arm, and this, of course, brings the left hand close to your collar, which enables you to secrete the coin in the recess between your neck and collar. So, you rub for a little while with the right hand and then show that the coin has disappeared.

You may think that the trick is too obvious to catch the audience, but if done well it misleads them absolutely. It is a classic case of misdirection. Just one word of warning: never repeat the trick in front of the same people. You cannot hope to delude the audience into thinking that the dropping of the coin was unintentional on a second occasion.

THREE-COIN TRICK

The idea behind this trick is to turn one coin into three, without any apparent means of palming or otherwise concealing the extra coins about one's person.

☞ You will need a small piece of wax and three 5p coins in your pocket. One of the coins should be new, the second should be a little worn and the third may be well worn and aged. Before announcing the trick, take the two well-worn coins, put a tiny piece of wax on each and press them upwards just under the edge of a table so that they are out of sight.

1. Show the new coin to your audience, roll up your sleeves and let everyone be sure that there is nothing concealed about your person.
2. Begin your patter along the lines that nothing is really solid – or so modern scientists tell us, and that by heat and friction you can turn one coin into three.

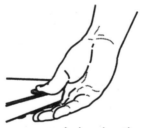

Two coins are concealed under the table edge

3. Place the coin on the table and press it with the ball of the thumb. Rub it about over the table a few times and work towards the edge, allowing the fingers to come under the edge and detach the second – partly worn – coin. Exhibit the two, showing that the first 5p is now a little worn and fatigued!
4. Repeat the performance rather more rapidly, and exhibit the three coins, pointing out that the first is now nearly worn away, although it is still good currency, and that the coin last produced is quite fresh and robust.

This trick needs good patter to create a convincing effect.

4.

Card tricks

To perform card tricks successfully demands a great deal of manual dexterity, and whole books are devoted to this branch of magic. However, any conjuror worth his or her salt can perform a few selected card tricks. The ones that follow either work themselves or rely on only basic sleight of hand.

FOUR JACKS

This is an easy trick to perform but one that is very effective, particularly if you can tell a good story. The four jacks are distributed throughout the pack, then magically reappear together on top.

1. The four jacks are taken from the pack and held up plainly in a fan for all to see. Behind these four cards, you hide four others. Having impressed on everybody that you are really showing them all the jacks and not kings or anything else, you place them on the top of the pack, which should be laid on the table face down in full view of everybody. So the four random cards are on the top, with the four jacks lying fourth to eighth.

Four random cards are hidden behind the fan of jacks

2. Now you start your story. 'Once upon a time, there were four burglars who entered a house and hid themselves in the attic. During the night, when everyone had gone to bed, one of them crept downstairs to the kitchen.' Take the top card – which the audience believes to be a jack – and place it at the bottom of the pack.

3. Continue: 'Then, the second burglar went silently down the stairs and entered the dining room on the second floor.' So saying, you slide the second card into the pack about three-quarters of the way down.

4. The story goes on: 'The third burglar thought it was time he did something, so off he went and crept into a bedroom on the second floor.' At this point you take the third card and put it into the pack about halfway down.

5. Continuing, you tell the audience about the fourth burglar. 'He started to go downstairs,' you say, as you place the fourth card about a quarter of the way down the pack. The audience now believes that you have hidden all four jacks throughout the pack.

6. Then, you change your whole tone. 'Suddenly, the master of the house, realising that there were intruders, rang the alarm bell.' On saying this, you bang your fist on the pack. 'The burglars were so frightened that they all rushed back into the attic.' Then, slowly and deliberately, you turn over the top four cards of the pack and show that the jacks really have come back.

Of course, when the four random cards were distributed through the pack, the jacks became numbers one to four.

CARD SHOWER

You will have to work on your dexterity for this trick, but once mastered it is very effective. You will be able to throw the whole pack into the air and yet to pluck out two chosen cards.

1. Hand a pack of cards to a spectator. Ask him to shuffle the pack thoroughly and then to name a card.
2. Take the pack back, run through it and find the selected card. Hand it to the spectator with the remark, 'Is this the card?' On being assured that it is, place it on the top of the pack.
3. Now ask a second person to name another card. Find it and after it has been confirmed as the chosen card, place it at the bottom of the pack.
4. Now you pretend to shuffle the pack, but what you actually do is to confine the shuffling to the central portion of the cards; the top and bottom cards stay in position.
5. Without attracting any attention, lick the thumb and index finger of your right hand. Grip the whole pack with them and at the same time slide the top and bottom cards a little off the pack, inwards towards your palm. Squeeze the pack to make the cards slide out of your grasp and, as they begin to fly, throw your hand upwards.

The effect is as though you have caught two flying cards

6. Up go the cards into the air and then they fall in a shower over your hand. When they lie scattered over the floor, two of them remain in your hand. They are the two cards selected by members of the audience.

The two chosen cards have remained in your hand because you licked your fingers; but, to the audience, it appears that while the cards were falling you were smart enough to single them out and catch them.

NAME THAT CARD

You can convince a friend that he knows more than he thinks he does, by the surreptitious application of simple logic.

1. Choose a card from the pack and put it face down on the table. You know what it is, but your friend has not seen it. In this example, let's say the card is the king of clubs. When you say to him, 'Of course, you know what card this is,' he will deny it. 'Oh yes, you do,' you say. 'I will prove to you that you do.' Then you proceed to question him.

2. First you ask, 'Do you prefer red or black cards?' If he replies red, you say, 'Right, that leaves the black cards.' Should he choose black, you say, 'Very good, I knew it.'

3. Next, ask, 'Now, of the black suits, which one is your favourite?' Again he can give two answers. If he favours clubs, you say, 'Of course,' and if he mentions spades you say, 'Good. That leaves clubs.'

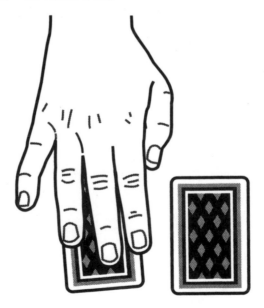

By a process of elimination, you will end up with the correct card

4. Now you continue by asking whether he likes court cards or number cards. Should he choose court cards, you reply with the remark that most people do. However, should he seem perverse and vote for the number cards, you point out that that leaves the court cards.

5. Your next question is as to whether he prefers a male or female among the court cards. If he opts for female, nod your head and say that this doesn't surprise you; and continue by remarking that if he prefers female cards, that leaves the male cards. On the other hand, should he choose male, agree with him, saying, 'I could see you were a man's man!' or some such.

6. Lastly, you say, 'Of the male court cards, do you like the old or the young?' If he says old, you point out that this means the king, and you turn over the chosen card and show it is the king of clubs. If he says he prefers the young, you point out that this leaves the king.

Any and every card in the pack may be singled out in exactly the same way – by a process of eliminating the unwanted cards. The curious thing about it all is that most people are very slow in understanding how they are made to choose the very card that is selected.

SELECTED CARD

This trick also works itself, the solution being found in the position of the cards.

1. Take twenty-five cards and allow a friend to shuffle and cut them as they please. Then lay them out in the following order:

1	2	3	4	5
6	7	8	9	10
11	12	13	14	15
16	17	18	19	20
21	22	23	24	25

2. Having done that, ask an onlooker to think of any card in the layout and to tell you in which horizontal row it is now resting. Carefully note the left-hand card at the end of the row indicated.
3. Next, pick up the cards, keeping them face up, but do it in this order. Take up card 1, place 6 on it and continue with 11, 16 and 21. Then follow 2, 7, 12, etc, to 25. As a card is lifted, be careful to place it on top of the others.
4. Now set out the cards once more in five horizontal rows. They will then take up these positions:

25	20	15	10	5
24	19	14	9	4
23	18	13	8	3
22	17	12	7	2
21	16	11	6	1

5. Once again ask the onlooker in which row the card he selected happens to be. When he tells you, look along the top or bottom row for the card that you noted at the left-hand

end of the row on the previous occasion. Above it or below it, vertically, in the row to which he now points, is the card he thought about.

6. Suppose 18 was the card thought about. The first time, your friend says, 'Row 4' and you look along to card 16. When the cards are relaid, he says 'Row 3'. You find card 16 and run up the vertical line until row 3 is reached. The card there is number 18.

LOST ACE

This trick is so easy to do and it is such a complete swindle! The four aces are shown and then hidden in the pack. Yet when an unsuspecting audience member looks for them, one has disappeared.

1. Take the ace of diamonds out of the pack and hide it somewhere in the room, perhaps under the clock, before your audience arrives.
2. Take the aces of hearts, clubs and spades from the pack, together with the 3 of diamonds. Hold them in your hand as shown below in an irregular manner, so that it looks as though you hold all four aces. By covering the two outer spots on the 3 of diamonds you can give the impression that this card is the fourth ace.
3. Invite your audience to look carefully at your hand, while you point in turn to each card and identify it as an ace. 'Now, watch as I slip each one separately into the pack,' you say, as you very deliberately place the four cards into various parts of the pack.
4. Ask a member of the audience to shuffle the entire pack thoroughly. Then ask a second person to come forwards and deal the cards with a view to recovering the four aces.

How to hold the four cards

5. The person selected takes the pack, deals from one end to the other and finds only three aces. One has mysteriously disappeared!

Express surprise and then reveal the missing ace in whatever way you like.

NAMING FOUR CARDS

This is a trick that works itself, as long as you deal out the cards correctly.

1. Take a pack of cards and let various people shuffle it. Then run off the four top cards. Ask a spectator to take them and remember one of them, forget all about the others and return the four to you.
2. Place the four cards face down on the table and deal off four more cards. Ask someone else to remember one of them, and proceed as before. Place the four cards on the top of the first four. Continue with two more sets of four cards and two more people.
3. When you have received sixteen cards in this way, deal them out face up, one card at a time, to give you four heaps of four. Deal one heap at a time.

The first card chosen will be the last card of the heap indicated

4. Then ask the person to whom you first gave cards to tell you in which heap his card now happens to be. Whichever heap he indicates, his card will be the last to be dealt of that heap.
5. In the case of the second, third and fourth people, their remembered cards will be the second, third and fourth cards from the top of the heaps they indicate.
6. Even if two people point to the same heap, the same rule applies.

5.

Challenging tricks

When you have mastered all the preceding tricks, you will naturally wish to try your hand at something a little more difficult. The following tricks are all more complicated, but the same basic principle applies: practise hard and they will soon be within your grasp.

Many of the tricks in this chapter require simple props. Inanimate objects can have a mind of their own, so don't attempt to perform these illusions before an audience until you are complete comfortable with the apparatus. If something does go wrong, use your patter to get out of it and move on to the next part of your act as quickly as possible!

MAGICAL CONE

You will often need a piece of apparatus for getting rid of a small article such as a watch, for instance. One of the simplest methods is with a paper cone, which you can make in front of your audience without fear of detection.

1. On your table lies a square sheet of white paper, which you roll into a cone. Into this the watch is dropped; but upon opening the paper cone later the article has vanished.
2. The secret is that the paper is actually two identical pieces glued together at their edges, and well pressed, so as to appear as one single sheet. One piece of paper has a cut running diagonally from side to side, as indicated by the dotted line in the figure below. This then forms a pocket.

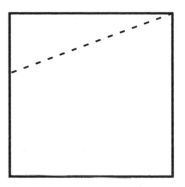

One sheet has a slit cut into it to create a pocket

3. Place one hand inside the cone, ostensibly to press out the dents, but really to open the pocket portion. This essential move looks quite natural, and does not raise the slightest suspicion.
4. The watch can now be placed inside this pocket and remain unnoticed, even when the cone is opened out.

By making the cone in front of your audience you are unlikely to make them suspicious.

SHOWER OF SWEETS

There is nothing in the world that will more quickly bring a conjuror into favour with his audience than a neatly executed distribution trick.

☞ You will need a piece of white linen, at the apex of which (A) is a curved pin. At the base of the triangle (BC) are two pieces of thin flat wire. D is filled with wrapped sweets, which cannot escape from the mouth of the triangular bag, owing to the presence of the wires.

☞ Thus loaded, the bag is put upon a ledge at the back of the your table, and the pin A is attached to the back edge of the tablecloth.

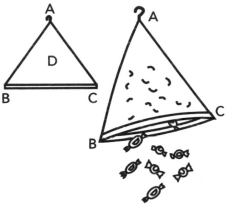

The fake needed to perform Shower of Sweets

1. A handkerchief is borrowed from the audience and is freely shown both sides.
2. Place the handkerchief on the table in such a way that the middle of it comes immediately over the bent pin A.
3. Pick up the handkerchief again, and at the same time pick up the sweets. They will not fall out until pressure is brought to bear upon the sides of the bag (AB and AC).

The resulting shower of sweets will be very popular with your audience.

MAGICAL DRAUGHT-BOARD

By some magic tearing, you can turn two sheets of paper – one black, one white – into a single sheet resembling a draught-board.

☞ You will need two sheets of black paper 50cm (20in) square. These are gummed together at their respective edges to create a pocket that is not noticeable at a short distance.

☞ Create another sheet in the pattern of a draught-board by pasting strips of black and white tissue paper together. Now fold this and secrete it within the pocket of the black sheets.

folded draught-board —

The fake draught-board is hidden in the pocket of the double sheet of black paper

1. To begin the trick, hold the black double sheet in your right hand (proclaiming it to be a single sheet) and a sheet of white paper in your left.
2. Place the two pieces of paper together and – apparently – tear them in half; then in half again. What you actually do is to take care not to tear the draught-board also, but to palm it, once the paper is torn sufficiently to enable you to do so.

3. Finally, roll the paper into a ball, which you compress between your palms.
4. Now open out the pieces of paper, smooth the creases away as far as possible, and reveal that the two colours have combined to create a draught-board.
5. When the draught-board is fully exhibited it is held at the two top corners by the right and left hands. In the palm of one hand you still hold a round ball of crumpled, torn paper.

The audience will see what they expect to see. Keep your palms towards you, just in case.

CUTTING THE HANDKERCHIEF

You borrow a handkerchief from the audience. You cut a piece off it and yet it remains intact. How is this done?

☛ The deception is provided by your magician's wand, which you modify as follows. The wand is a black tube, inside of which is a wire spring, attached to one end. This wire passes through the tube and, at the far end, which is open, it grips a small piece of white material.

☛ The spring would normally pull the white material up the tube, but, to prevent this, the point of a nail is soldered to the inside of the tube and the material is hooked on to it.

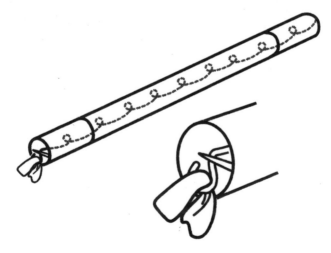

Modifying a magic wand

1. Borrow a handkerchief from an unsuspecting audience member. Take your wand from your magician's table and wrap the handkerchief partially around it.
2. Now with a pair of scissors, cut off a little piece and hold it up for all to see. Instead of cutting the handkerchief, you take hold of the tip of the material in the tube, pull it out, cut off a small section, and, on letting go, the remainder bounds up the inside of the tube, out of sight.
3. Every member of the audience, with one exception, will find this extremely amusing. When the laughter has subsided, snatch the handkerchief from the wand and hold it up by two corners to show that it is intact. The audience is dumbfounded.
4. So what happens to the piece that was cut? It is only a very small piece, and, while you are unfolding the handkerchief, you roll it into a ball and drop it down your sleeve.

When performed well, this is a very effective trick; accordingly, you should practise it over and over again before presenting it to an audience.

HANDKERCHIEF ILLUSION

You demonstrate to your audience that the glass tube in your hand is quite empty. Then suddenly it is filled with a silk handkerchief! A suitable tube can be bought from a magic shop.

☞ Before you begin this trick, you must conceal a neatly folded silk handkerchief under the lapel of your jacket. If you pat it down well and are careful, it will not need securing.

☞ To one end of the handkerchief is fixed a fine silk thread, which passes from the handkerchief, through the tube and down to a button on the front of your trousers. There must be some slack, so that you can move the tube about while you are emphasising the fact that it is quite empty.

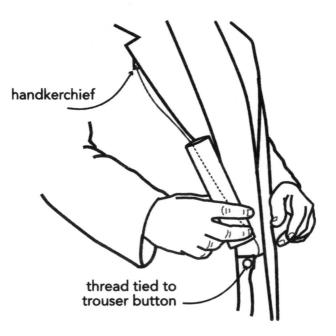

The starting position for Handkerchief Illusion

72

1. Stand a little way from the audience, and in your right hand hold a fairly wide glass tube. Emphasise that it is quite empty.
2. Now make a sudden movement, which dislodges the handkerchief. You rush the tube towards it, and it can do nothing else but enter the tube. It cannot come out at the other end, because your hand is in the way.
3. When you see that things have happened as you required, a sharp wrench breaks the thread and the clue to the mystery is destroyed.

The length of the thread must be right and will depend on your height and length of arm.

ALL-A-GROWING

If there is anything in the world that ought to be distrusted it is the sleeve of the conjuror. At least, you will think so after following this trick.

☛ Before you begin this trick, secrete a bunch of artificial flowers up your sleeve. You will also need a paper cylinder that fits over your arm.

1. Show an empty paper cylinder to the audience. Pass it round for them to look through, and to emphasise the fact that it really is empty, and does not merely look empty, you put your hand and part of your sleeve through it.

2. Of course, you say, it is uncomfortable to have a paper cylinder around your arm, so you pull it off and look round your table for somewhere to put it. Your table is, naturally, crowded with various objects and a place is not easily found. But there is a flower vase with no flowers in it standing on the table, right in front of the audience. For want of a better place to put the cylinder, you drop it over the vase.

The flowers are revealed when the cylinder is lifted from the vase

3. 'Hang on a minute,' you say in surprise. 'What's this?' You immediately lift off the cylinder – and there is the vase, containing a nice bunch of flowers!

4 When you take the cylinder off your sleeve, you move the flowers into the vase, ready to be revealed a moment later.

An astute audience may well guess how this is done, but will nonetheless enjoy it.

MAGIC WHISTLE

This is one of those silly tricks that cause a good deal of consternation. The props can be bought from a magic shop.

☛ You will need to tie a whistle to the end of your wand.

☛ In your left hand hold a rubber bulb, which is joined to a length of tubing that travels up your arm and goes into one of the pockets of your waistcoat. Here it is fixed to the tip of a second whistle. When you squeeze the bulb, the whistle sounds.

1. Stand up before your audience, holding a wand in your hand, which you are careful to point out has magic properties. Explain that tied to the wand is a very ordinary whistle. In order to show that there is absolutely no deception, you pass round the wand and the whistle for examination.

2. Now ask somebody to put a question, the answer to which is known to everybody. The answer must take the form of 'yes' or 'no'; for example, 'Is an elephant bigger than a cockroach?' or, 'Are we in Prague?'

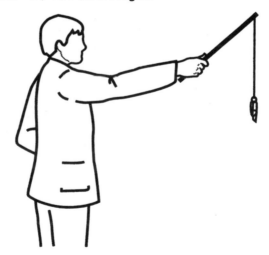

The whistle sound comes from your pocket, not your wand

3. Before proceeding further you explain that when the answer is No the magic wand will cause the whistle to blow once, but when the answer is Yes it will blow twice.
4. Someone puts the question, 'Do shrimps sing in their sleep?' and the whistle gives one shrill blast. This is followed by 'Ought animals to be kind to their young?' Two blasts are heard. In this way the answers to five or six questions are given correctly, much to the enjoyment of the company.
5. Of course, it is the whistle in your pocket that makes the noise, not the one at the end of the string. Be very careful to smother the air hole of the whistle as little as possible, or muffled blasts will be given and will cause suspicion.

Always stand a few paces away from the nearest spectator so that the distance between the two whistles cannot be appreciated.

TORN PAPER

How is it that a piece of paper signed by a member of your audience can be torn up and yet reappear, undamaged, moments later? The secret is, of course, in the planning.

☛ Take two sheets of paper 20cm (8in) square, one of which has a projecting corner (which is cut off before the trick starts).

☛ Fold one of the sheets into three rows of three to give nine squares and paste the middle square to the middle of the other sheet. Iron them flat.

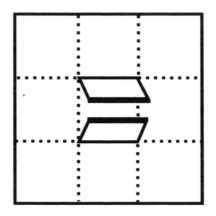

Preparing the paper for Torn Paper

1   Announce that you need an odd piece of paper for your next trick and pick one up 'at random' from your table. Of course, you actually select your prepared prop. Make a show of trimming away the excess with scissors, so that it is right for your purpose.

2. Now ask a volunteer from the audience to come and sign their initials in the middle of the paper. When he comes forward, you rest the magic sheet on a folded newspaper and he signs. The newspaper disguises the thickness of the paper.

3. Now, turning to the audience and holding up the paper, you advise everybody to watch carefully. Then, slowly and deliberately, you tear the sheet into three vertical strips which you place one behind the other.

4. Next you tear the strips, all together, into three equal squares. 'You all saw me tear the paper now, didn't you?' you remark, 'and you all saw that it was the sheet signed by this lady.' When everybody nods an assent, you turn and walk towards the table, taking the opportunity to palm the odd pieces of paper.

5. The torn sheet has a full-size folded sheet behind it that masquerades as the original sheet when opened out. Naturally, it bears the necessary signature, as the sheets are stuck together. So you are able to turn round again and unfold what you have in your hand. It is the complete sheet, untorn and bearing the volunteer's signature.

DIVINING NUMBERS

If you have a head for figures, this numerical puzzle can provide a brief but bewildering diversion.

1. To divine someone's age, ask your volunteer to:
    ☞ Write down the number of the month in which her birthday occurs
    ☞ Double the number
    ☞ Add 5 to the latter
    ☞ Multiply the answer by 50
    ☞ Add to this her age
    ☞ Subtract the number of days there are in an ordinary year from the above
    ☞ Read out aloud the figures arrived at in this way
    ☞ To the answer she supplies, you quickly add 115, without divulging what you are doing and then the last total is split up as follows; the two figures on the extreme right of the total indicate her age and the remaining figures, the number of the month in which her birthday occurs.

2. Work through the following examples for practice:

Number of birth month	5	12
Double it	10	24
Add 5	15	29
Multiply by 50	750	1,450
Add age		
(6 in the first case, 29 in the second)	756	1,479
Subtract 365	391	1,114
You add 115	506	1,229

3. Thus, in the first case the age is 6 (the nought does not affect the answer) and the birth month is 5, May. In the second case the age is 29 and the birth month is 12, December. Note that no number to be guessed should be over 90.

There are, of course, several different ways of working problems of this kind, but the method cited here is recommended because there is no apparent connection between the final number, read out by the volunteer, and the figures that you supply. Thus, in the second case above the volunteer calls out 1,114 and you promptly tell him that he was born in December and that his age is 29.

CHANGING PLACES

This is a very pretty experiment to perform before an audience that has some pretensions to being scientific. It takes a rather long time, and therefore it is advisable to do the preliminary part and set the glasses to one side while other things are happening. Then you can return to it.

☛ You will need two wine glasses of the same dimensions.

☛ Note that when the glasses are inverted, you will require them to hold water. Therefore, it is not sufficient for the lips to rest in contact – they must adhere. This is only possible when the edges are ground flat and smeared with petroleum jelly.

☛ To grind them, rub gently in a circular direction on a smooth surface of emery paper. Mind that it is smooth and level, or the glass will crack during the process.

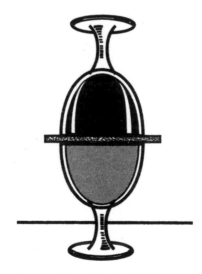

The water and the claret will change places

1. To perform the experiment, fill one prepared glass with water and the other with claret, which will still be drinkable when we have done with it.
2. On the glass of water, rest a thin sheet of metal gauze that is perfectly flat and free from buckles. Press it down on to the greased lip to ensure suction; then put a piece of glass on top of the gauze.
3. Invert the glass of water and rest it exactly over the glass of wine, so that the two are in perfect contact. Slide away the sheet of glass and see that no water falls out nor air rushes in.
4. If you have performed this experiment properly, and have managed to keep both the glasses quite full of liquid, a very curious thing happens. In less than a quarter of an hour, the water and wine will have changed places. The water will be underneath and the wine on top.

Why does this happen? It's basic physics. The claret is less dense than the water. Accordingly the water that you put on top must find its way into the bottom glass.

USEFUL BOWLER HAT

A bowler hat should form part of every conjuror's kit, since it can be used in several ways. This trick is a complete swindle!

☛ Prepare a bowler hat. Cut a small hole in the side so that with the inner band turned up and the exterior silk hatband moved away you will be able to see inside.

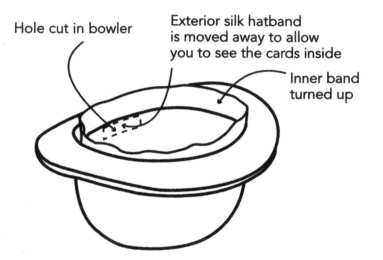

Hole cut in bowler

Exterior silk hatband is moved away to allow you to see the cards inside

Inner band turned up

You can easily see what is in the hat

1. Present a pack of cards to your audience and ask for five cards to be selected. When this has been done, tell your friends to stack the selected cards so that you cannot see what they are, and then hold out your bowler for somebody to put them into it.
2. You now hold the bowler just above your eye-level, and so that your view shall be masked, you lift up the inside lining. This makes an additional screen, which effectively prevents you from seeing over the top of the brim.

3. At this point you say, 'I will now give you the 3 of diamonds,' or whatever, and sure enough, you pick out the correct card. You repeat this until all the five cards have been correctly named and drawn out of the hat.
4. You lift up the inner band, ostensibly to screen your view, and, unseen by the audience you push the hatband out of the way while holding the hat. Thus you can look through the peephole at the cards in the hat.

The cards will need to be face up in the hat.

MAGIC TUBE

You show your audience that a tube is empty yet you magically produce a silk handkerchief from it.

☛ You will need to make a simple piece of apparatus from three short lengths of cardboard rolls, the narrowest being about 2.5cm (1in) in diameter, the second a little wider to fit over it and the third a little wider still to fit over the second roll.

☛ From the second or middle-sized roll cut a length of about 15cm (6in) and paste on the outside a piece of thin, brightly patterned paper. From the third or widest roll cut two rings as shown at A in the figure below.

☛ A piece of tissue paper is seen at B covering one end of the tube and held in position by one of the rings. Another piece of tissue paper is to be held in position by the other ring, at the other end of the tube.

☛ The section of carton shown at C in the diagram is constructed by cutting from the narrowest roll a length of about 10cm (4in) and to one end affixing a conical shape constructed from stiff brown paper. This section must be able to go easily into the outer tube without protruding at either end.

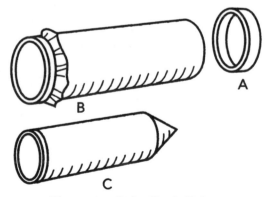

The parts of the Magic Tube

☛ The handkerchief is loaded into this carton and the end closed by sticking on a paper disc. The carton should be painted flesh colour on the outside.

1. To perform the trick, make a big show of demonstrating that there is nothing in the tube.
2. Close each end with tissue paper, fastening them with the rings. Meanwhile palm the inner carton and while manipulating the empty outer tube press the pointed end of the inner carton through one of the paper discs of the former, any damage to which is covered by the duplicate on the end of the inner carton.
3. Break open the end of the tube opposite to the pointed end of the inner carton and produce the handkerchief with panache.

You will need to be very competent at palming to perform this trick successfully.

MY THUMB

This trick always goes down well with small children, but the grown-ups usually laugh, too.

☛ You will need an imitation thumb, obtainable from good magic shops. Attach a piece of elastic to it and carry the other end of the elastic to the side of your waistcoat.

1. Stand in front of the audience and stretch out your left hand, sideways. Stick out the thumb prominently and pointing downwards.
2. Without causing any fuss, take the imitation thumb in the palm of the right hand, where it is unseen, and approach the right hand towards the left.
3. Suddenly, grab at the thumb of the left hand with the fingers of the right and, at the same time, jerk the left thumb behind the rest of the hand. If done carefully it can be entirely hidden, leaving a very prominent joint.
4. Then slowly bring the right hand away and open it towards the audience. There is the missing thumb!

Children will believe that the thumb in your right hand belongs on your left

5. After that, you reverse the process. The right hand, with loose thumb very evident, approaches the left hand and, with a sudden click, you pretend to replace the severed member. What you do is to jerk the real thumb back into sight and release your hold of the imitation thumb, which shoots out of view in the folds of your waistcoat because of the elastic. Then you open the outstretched right hand and, of course, there is no surplus thumb in it.

With practice, this looks very realistic indeed.

BALANCING A WINE GLASS ON A PLAYING CARD

Who would have thought that you could balance a glass on a card? It's easy when you know how.

☛ You will need two playing cards, one an exact duplicate of the other. One of the cards should be modified to include a back strut. Keep this card hidden on your table.

The wine glass is sitting on a modified card

1. To begin the trick, take the unmodified card from a pack and hold it up for inspection. Then go to your table and pour wine into a glass until it is three-quarters full.
2. Exercise some sleight of hand so that you swap the straight card for the trick one. With great aplomb, stand the glass on the edge of the card and hold it out at arm's length. Your performance will be sure to meet with applause.
3. By opening the strut, you have not a two-way but a three-way support, and the glass is easily balanced. Of course, the strut must be hidden from the audience.

You should suggest that it is the weight of the glass of wine that keeps the card from falling.

MYSTIC NAIL

A box of ordinary household nails is given for examination, and then, after one has been selected by the audience for use, the conjuror passes it through his finger. Upon withdrawal of nail, the said finger is found to be absolutely free from injury, and the nail may be passed round for further inspection.

☞ You will need a fake nail, below, available from magic shops.

Palmed genuine nail

A fake nail – and how to use it

1. The box of nails offered for inspection contains the same sort as the fake one, which you hold in the palm of your right hand. Hold the box of nails in the same hand, so that the fake cannot be seen. A nail has been chosen, and you return to your table in order to put down the box. At an opportune moment, put the fake around your finger while at the same time the genuine nail is securely held under the cover of thumb, second, third and fourth fingers.
2. After facing the audience and making dreadful faces and groaning as if in great pain, you again turn towards your table, ostensibly to pick up a small tray, but in reality to give you the opportunity to palm the fake nail. The real nail is allowed to drop on to the tray and then once more handed round for minute inspection.

The more over-the-top your 'agony', the better.

BUNCH OF FLOWERS

This trick relies on the purchase of special magician's props.

☞ You need a canister with two lids, one at either end, and two compartments separated by a diagonal division running almost the entire length of the canister. You will also need some magician's flowers.

1. Such a canister is shown to the audience and proved to be empty. Into it is placed a handkerchief. The lid is put on and a few extravagant passes made with the hands. Upon the removal of the lid, the handkerchief has vanished into thin air, and in its place some lovely spring flowers are to be seen.

There is a handkerchief at one end of the canister – and a bunch of flowers at the other

2. The figure shows the secret. The handkerchief is placed in one compartment whilst, before the show started, some specially made conjuring flowers were put into the other. Their petals are made of varicoloured tissue paper, and the leaves of green silk. Each flower has a spring in it, so that when collapsed they take up very little room; but when allowed to expand, they spread out in a most wonderful fashion.

In order to effect a change of any kind, you need only turn the canister upside-down while returning to your table.

Index